A baby
called John

Story by Penny Frank

Illustrated by John Hayson

THE LION
STORY BIBLE

31

TRING · BELLEVILLE · SYDNEY

T he Bible tells us how God sent his Son Jesus to show us what God is like and to tell us how we can belong to God's kingdom.
This is the story of when John the Baptist was born. He was the cousin of Jesus. God was going to use him to prepare the people to listen to Jesus. You can find the story in your Bible in Luke's Gospel, chapter 1.

Copyright © 1984 Lion Publishing
Published by
Lion Publishing plc
Icknield Way, Tring, Herts, England
ISBN 0 85648 756 2
Lion Publishing Corporation
10885 Textile Road, Belleville,
Michigan 48111, USA
ISBN 0 85648 756 2
Albatross Books
PO Box 320, Sutherland, NSW 2232, Australia
ISBN 0 86760 540 5

First edition 1984

Printed and bound in Hong Kong
by Mandarin Offset International (HK) Ltd.

British Library Cataloguing in
Publication Data
Frank, Penny
A baby called John. – (The Lion
Story Bible; 31)
1. John, *the Baptist, Saint* – Juvenile
literature
I. Title   II. Hayson, John
232.9'4   BS2456

ISBN 0-85648-756-2

There was once an old man in Israel
called Zechariah. His wife's name was
Elizabeth. Everyone knew Zechariah
because he was a priest in the temple.

Zechariah and Elizabeth often talked together about God.

'I like the old stories of when God spoke face to face with people like Moses and Samuel,' said Zechariah. 'I would love to hear him speaking to me in the temple.'

'I like the old stories of the miracles God did for Sarah and Hannah,' said Elizabeth. 'If only he would give me a baby too.'

Zechariah and Elizabeth were old. They had never had any children.

One day there was great excitement at Zechariah's home. He had been chosen out of all the priests for a special duty in the temple.

Zechariah would pray for Israel inside the temple. Elizabeth and all the other people would wait outside and pray.

Zechariah left all the people outside in the sunshine. He walked slowly into the cool temple.

Suddenly he saw a bright light.
Zechariah was very frightened. He was
all alone. What was happening?

Then an angel from God spoke to Zechariah. 'Don't be afraid, Zechariah. God does still talk to people, and I have come to tell you that he still does miracles too. You and Elizabeth are going to have a baby. You are to call him John.

'When he grows up John will be a very special man. He will tell the people to get ready for God's Son,' said the angel.
  'I must be dreaming,' said Zechariah. 'We're much too old to have a baby.'

'Don't you know how great God is?'
said the angel. 'Because you would not
believe, you will not be able to speak
until the baby is born. You'll find out
then that I have told you the truth.'

Elizabeth did not know why Zechariah
was taking such a long time in the
temple.

When at last he came out, all the
people knew that something had
happened, because Zechariah could not
speak.

When they got home, Zechariah had to write down what had happened so that Elizabeth could understand. They were both very excited.

They started to count the weeks until the baby would be born.

While they were waiting, Elizabeth had a visit from her cousin Mary. Mary was waiting for her own baby to be born.

Mary and Elizabeth were so excited.
They had not seen each other for a
long time.

Elizabeth told Mary how the angel
had spoken to Zechariah in the temple.

Mary said to Elizabeth, 'The angel came to me too.'

They were amazed that God was sending such special babies to ordinary people.

Then Mary went back home to Joseph.

At last the day came. Elizabeth's baby was born. He really was beautiful.

All the family and friends came to see him. 'Can we cuddle baby Zechariah?' they asked.

'His name is not Zechariah,' said Elizabeth. 'His name is John. But he does love being cuddled.'

'That's silly,' the relations said. 'He should be called Zechariah. The first son is always called by his father's name.'

Then Zechariah wrote out a message
for them all to read.
  'HIS NAME IS JOHN,' it said.

As soon as he had written the message and obeyed what the angel of God had told him, Zechariah started to speak again.

Zechariah really enjoyed telling
everyone about what had happened.

They all looked again at the new baby.
They nodded wisely.

'That is a very special baby,' they
said. 'When he grows up John will have
special work to do for God.'

The Lion Story Bible is made up of 52 individual stories for young readers, building up an understanding of the Bible as one story – God's story – a story for all time and all people.

The New Testament section (numbers 31-52) covers the life and teaching of God's Son, Jesus. The stories are about the people he met, what he did and what he said. Almost all we know about the life of Jesus is recorded in the four Gospels – Matthew, Mark, Luke and John. The word gospel means 'good news'.
 The last four stories in this section are about the first Christians, who started to tell others the 'good news', as Jesus had commanded them – a story which continues today all over the world.

The story of *A baby called John* comes from the New Testament, Luke's Gospel chapter 1. Long before, through his special spokesmen, the Old Testament prophets, God had promised he would send a Saviour to rescue his people. But before his work could begin, people had to be prepared. So John was sent to tell people that God's King was coming, to call them to change their ways and do as God wanted. From before the time of John's birth it was clear that he was to be a very special person.
 The next book in the series, number 32: *The first Christmas,* tells the most famous story of all time, the birth of Jesus.